Beloved Educators
Women of Color Who Inspire Us

Penelope E. Lattimer
Valarie W. French
Marilyn C. Maye
L. Debra Napier
Mary McGriff
Doris R. Lee

Publisher's Cataloging-in-Publication
(Provided by Quality Books, Inc.)

Lattimer, Penelope E.
   Beloved educators: women of color who inspire us /
   Penelope E. Lattimer, Valarie W. French, Marilyn C.
   Maye, L. Debra Napier, Mary McGriff, Doris R. Lee.
      pages cm
      ISBN-13: 978-1496154729
      ISBN-10: 149615472X

   1. African American women teachers--Interviews.
   2. African American women teachers--United States—
   History --20th century. 3. Urban schools--United
   States-- History--20th century.   I. Title.

LA2311.L38 2014   370'.922
                    QBI14-600069

Praise for "Beloved Educators"

Beloved Educators makes evident the profound influences that family and community life in childhood and adolescence have on later professional accomplishment and commitment. How powerful is the message of hope and belief when the odds of success are so long! With hindsight it is not surprising that these women viewed careers as teachers and educators as "sacred work." Each of them tells us that if one begins with a belief that all children can learn and want to learn, then there is no excuse as a teacher or administrator for settling for less than that. And, if you have these beliefs and achieve the kinds of remarkable successes documented in the book, why stop? For these women, "social justice" in education was a life calling leading to decades of service and accomplishment. The book is recommended for prospective teachers and especially for in-service professionals. My guess is that those who have the inclination and potential to become "beloved educators," will find inspiration and additional motivation to persevere.
Richard DeLisi
Dean & Professor, Graduate School of Education
Rutgers, The State University of New Jersey

Beloved Educators reminds us that perseverance, commitment, resilience, and love are the foundation of good teaching. This powerful and insightful book takes us on a journey through the lives of African American women who despite facing personal sacrifice, discrimination, and ongoing inequalities had a significant impact on the lives of the children they taught and the educators who followed in their footsteps. These women show what it means to truly honor our commitment to our children. Whether you are considering a career in teaching or you are a veteran educator, *Beloved Educators* is a 'must read' that will move and inspire you.

Crystal M. Edwards
Superintendent,
Lawrence Township (NJ) Public School District

Beloved Educators points the way for educators seeking to understand the values, dispositions, and skills needed to ensure that every child has the opportunity to succeed in school. The rich portraits of seven goal-oriented African American women educators capture the stories of women who refused to permit race, gender or bias to prevent them from doing whatever was required to achieve career success, and to provide every student with the tools to achieve socially, emotionally, culturally and academically.
Each memoir is thoughtfully crafted with details of their struggles and the strategies they implemented to succeed in classrooms, schools, districts, and institutions of higher education. The wisdom of these women is particularly relevant to contemporary challenges associated with meeting the needs of children who depend upon teachers, principals, and professors to achieve success in schools, family and community. Their stories embed core values and knowledge needed for present and future generations of educators to serve children well.

Larry Leverett
Executive Director, Panasonic Foundation

Beloved Educators is a clear and powerful account of African American women who triumphed through difficult times and circumstances to serve many children and families as their teachers. Above all, these teachers are models of what is possible, regardless of obstacles. This story of these wonderful women must be told and remembered.

William Librera
Former New Jersey State Commissioner of Education

It is hard to imagine the impact of the seven grand women whose lives are portrayed in this book on the thousands of young people they nurtured. Their students will, of course, carry a little of each of their teachers with them always, but now, we too, can share in their stories, admiring the struggles and the triumphs that characterized their lives. As we honor these seven women, we too, become their students, carrying from the book a little more about what it is, was, and forever will be, to become a great teacher.

Willa Spicer
Former Deputy Commissioner, NJ Department of Education

If we are fortunate, we remember the teachers who changed our lives, the ones without whom we could never have become who we are. My third-grade teacher, Mrs. Florida Kelly, was my "beloved educator." This book's stories are about women like her. Some have national reputations; others are leaders in their local communities. All of their narratives are instructive and inspiring. If you are a teacher, you will find practical lessons as well as encouragement here. If you have ever loved a teacher, you will want to thank her again after reading this book.

Cheryl A. Wall
Zora Neale Hurston Professor of English
Rutgers, The State University of New Jersey

DEDICATION

To education - the profession that prepares
all other professions - and to compassionate
educators worldwide

ACKNOWLEDGEMENTS

Thank you to the women profiled here who generously gave of their time and graciously shared their stories.

Thank you to Jennifer Hanson for her encouraging comments and for editing the original manuscript.

Thank you to "the glue" of the Rutgers Institute for Improving Student Achievement, Carrie Harris and Olivia Walker, for their editorial assistance and unwavering support in bringing this book to life.

Beloved Educators

Table of Contents

Introduction

Education is for improving the lives of others and for leaving your community and world better than you found it.

Marian Wright Edelman

What does it mean to be a teacher? What happens after you have chosen as a profession to improve the lives of other people's children? Will you grow along the way? Will you change? Will you find joy? Will you persevere? How will you deal with the successes, as well as with the challenges? When you look back at the end of your career, what will stand out? To answer these questions we often look for role models. We learn by watching those around us who by their achievements -- big and small -- show us a way forward. Beloved educators are the teachers, the role models, who have by their example, whether intentionally or unintentionally, directly or indirectly, inspire us.

On the surface the women profiled here would seem to have little in common; they were born in different places, in different decades, and into different circumstances. They came to teaching along different paths and their careers followed different trajectories. Some worked in the same district for many years, while others gained national prominence. These differences make each woman's story unique.

However, beneath the surface there are striking similarities that reveal some of the triumphs, as well as shared challenges, of African American women in public education. Each of these women faced obstacles and each responded with courage, persistence and a conviction in the power of one voice to address systemic inequalities. Dorothy Strickland said, "I have been guided by a strong belief that it is important for me to do the very best job I can... and then give a little bit more." Several began their teaching careers in de jure segregated schools in the south, and others taught in de facto segregated schools in northern cities. Two recounted facing white parents who were surprised to see an African American woman in front of the classroom. Each has had to learn to balance the exhilaration of helping students achieve with personal disappointments and professional isolation.

As these women have been role models and inspirations for us, each woman credits a teacher as the inspiration for her own teaching style and philosophy. Whether from elementary or high school, memories of these "beloved educators" still evoke fond smiles. As Bessie Wade recalled, "Walking with [my 2nd grade teacher] everyday [to and from school] was very special. She inspired me to be an educator." But, even before going to school, each woman credits a parent as her first role model. Whether a father, a mother, or a grandparent, there was someone in the home saying: if you prepare, if you work hard, if you do your best – then you can accomplish anything! Lillie Ham Hendry's parents said it simply and directly: "Don't ever let me catch you idle." Parents also set examples for community involvement and religious faith that each woman described as still an important part of her identity today.

Each woman carried these early lessons into her own practice, most notably by setting and maintaining high expectations for students. Doreen Hall observed, "This is how educators in the great cities make the critical difference. We change the children who are personally defenseless. Their only way out is their teacher." These women were mission-driven, that is, most of them entered public education as a 'calling' rather than a career. All of them earned advanced degrees and each spoke to the importance of being a life-long learner in order to be a better educator. Each stated a belief that all children can learn if they are given opportunities, and talked about her deeply felt, personal commitment to helping African American students succeed. Interestingly, although their teaching situations, approaches, and content areas varied, all of them described experiential and performance based teaching and learning as integral to students' growth and development. Jean Tunstall recalled, "I liked exposing students to another way of life." Penelope Lattimer said, "Informal learning, experiential learning, is the kind of thing I really believe in. Experiential learning, motivational learning, [is] being in an environment in which you really have to do some critical thinking, when you have to make decisions and apply knowledge that isn't strictly right and wrong."

For all of their accomplishments each woman asks to be remembered simply as someone who made a difference in the lives of students. Evelyn Crawford summed up more than 30 years of classroom teaching this way: "You have to work and plan and expect from children every day. You have to value each child. Work with whatever that child brings to you because when you do there will always be a way to get that child to learn."

We must not, in trying to think about how we can make a big difference, ignore the small daily differences we can make which, over time, add up to big differences that we often cannot foresee.

Marian Wright Edelman

Evelyn Crawford

By Mary McGriff

Growing up as the daughter of an elementary school teacher, I always thought I understood what it meant to say, "My mother is a teacher." Yet, it was not until I had the opportunity to interview her that I began to comprehend fully the many ways in which Evelyn Crawford enriched the lives of others.

A plain and seemingly obvious statement can sometimes reflect a reality that is far more intricate and profound. Evelyn Crawford describes her 33-year career as, "Teaching. Just teaching." When asked to elaborate, she provides equally matter-of-fact answers that suggest, "I did my job, as any good teacher would. What's more to say?" Yet, when the focus of our discussion shifts away from her and onto her own teachers and students, Evelyn offers an abundance of rich reflections about her schooling and her years of teaching in segregated Mississippi and in New Jersey during the years following the 1967 riots. As Evelyn speaks about her career, she speaks about responsibility and empathy, as well as high expectations for herself and for those in her charge. As she speaks, the essence of "just teaching" resolves itself into a profile of a truly transformative teacher.

In 1940, Evelyn began first grade at George Washington Carver School in rural Century, Florida. During her early years, she learned what it meant for teachers to take a personal interest in their students. She recalls the personal attention she received from her fifth-grade teacher, Mrs. Collins: "I got a chance to go home with Mrs. Collins to spend a weekend in the city of Pensacola. Several teachers came from Pensacola, and they would do this with students every now and then. I remember going to the market with Mrs. Collins. She took me along with her to stop in on her neighbors and relatives. We went to the beach because she knew that I wanted to see the ocean. And so, I got a chance to be exposed to some city living which I could not have done had it not been for my teacher." Taking an interest in students' lives and interests was a lesson that would benefit Evelyn's classes for the next three decades.

Evelyn's schooling also included examples of effective teaching, such as that done by Mrs. Jones, her high school algebra teacher: "Mrs. Jones was the kind of teacher that, if you didn't understand how to do something, you were never afraid to let that be known. And frankly speaking, she was the kind of teacher who could tell when students did not understand because she had us work at the board. We were always involved in our learning that way. She knew who needed more help, and she gave it. That is something I remembered."

Evelyn graduated from Alabama A&M College, a land grant institution established to educate Negroes in technical skills. Following her May 1955 graduation, she obtained her first teaching position—a fourth grade class at the M. F. Nichols School in Biloxi, Mississippi. Her first classroom was meagerly equipped, as was common for the classrooms of black students in the Jim Crow[1] south. There were desks, chairs, one blackboard, and textbooks for reading and arithmetic. Field trips were unheard of, as were art or music instruction. Having grown up under this system of segregation and constraint, however, Evelyn did not view these limitations as permanent barriers to advancement. Rather, she saw them as normal conditions that could be transcended through classroom teaching. So, as she commenced her career, she recalls feeling nervousness, excitement, and above all, a profound sense of responsibility for increasing her students' knowledge.

In Biloxi, Evelyn boarded with relatives of a family friend, and she recalls that the twenty minutes she spent walking home from school each day provided valuable time for reflecting on that day's lessons and for thinking about tomorrow's teaching.

---

[1] **Jim Crow laws** were state and local laws in the United States that mandated *de jure* racial segregation in all public facilities in southern states of the former Confederacy. Jim Crow laws legalized the segregation of public schools, public places, and public transportation, and the segregation of restrooms, restaurants, and drinking fountains for blacks.

Opportunities for mentoring were limited, and improving her teaching skills was a self-directed experience. "As a first year teacher, you scrambled for yourself," she recalls. "You used whatever educational materials and magazines and books you could find to get ideas from. There was the *Teacher* magazine and the *Instructor* magazine. These were two magazines that I bought for myself, and I got ideas and methods from those. In the hall I might notice another teacher's procedure for lining up her students, and I figured that was something I could do also. Trial. Error. Thinking about what worked. Thinking about how to improve. Again, those walks home were very helpful for such thinking."

Responsibility clearly translated into high expectations for herself, but to Evelyn, responsibility also meant holding consistently high expectations for her students. She believed that high expectations served as a powerful learning tool for black children in the Jim Crow south because those expectations impacted all aspects of her students' lives. Children were expected to contribute to their family's economic survival by caring for younger siblings or by pitching in with farm work. Proper conduct was demanded in church and other public places, and all members of the black community did their part to uphold such standards for all children. As a result, it was natural to hold children to high standards in school, and Evelyn credits this as the critical factor that enabled children to achieve in spite of the systematic limitations that segregation presented.

"You expected the children to work towards learning how to multiply, to work towards learning how to write a sentence, to work towards learning a verb from a noun. You expected this, and the consistency of children knowing that they were expected to do this was so very important. It was nothing for a parent to come and look in the window to see what her child was doing. Being in a segregated situation, the children knew you cared. They knew you cared, and they knew that the caring extended to the whole community."

Not long into her teaching career, Evelyn married and moved to New Jersey. Her husband was enrolled in a master's degree program at nearby New York University, and Evelyn continued her work with elementary school children. With this move, she left legalized segregation behind, yet the effects of racial discrimination would continue to impact her teaching.

In the 1960s Plainfield, New Jersey, was a racially-divided city that was controlled by an all-white city council, a white mayor, and a white police force. Over time, disparity of economic opportunity turned some of Plainfield's black neighborhoods into blighted ghettos, and also created a tinderbox of suppressed frustration. Evelyn joined the staff of Emerson Elementary School in September 1967—two months after the black community's pent-up anger ignited, leading to two days of fire-setting, looting, and police skirmishes. This was also Plainfield's second year into a desegregation plan that reorganized existing neighborhood elementary schools into citywide grade-level schools. Emerson was the city's school for fifth and sixth grade students. As a result, Evelyn taught black and white fifth grade children who were bussed from different pockets of the city and whose neighborhoods were still reeling from the aftershocks of the previous summer's riots.

With this as the backdrop, one might expect Evelyn's earliest years of teaching in Plainfield to reflect some of the anger, fear, and frustration that black and white families felt during these years. While she recognized the fact that most of her students' families did not support the dissolution of neighborhood schools, she found parents of both races to be positive and supportive of their children's classroom learning experiences. She notes, "A lot happened in Plainfield the year before I arrived. Every now and then I would overhear a student saying, 'My father thinks it's silly for me to have to come all the way over here to go to school.' But there was no evidence of all that racial tension among the children. At conferences or when we had school events, white parents were every bit as positive about their children's learning as were the black parents. We basically focused on school. It was: what skills do fifth graders need to leave my room knowing?"

As the 1960s gave way to the 1970s, however, Evelyn recognized a growing pattern of underachievement among students in her classes. The white families who chose to remain in Plainfield following the 1967 riots now tended to enroll their children in private or parochial schools. By 1978, the district had chosen to return to its neighborhood districting model since there were no longer enough white children attending public school to justify bussing, and Emerson once again became a kindergarten to fifth grade school.

That year, 1978, also marked the inaugural year of New Jersey's Minimum Basic Skills Testing program. Evelyn's principal assigned her to teach the school's third grade basic skills class. This class was for a group of struggling learners who needed intensive remediation in order to pass the test. Evelyn's persistent emphasis on skill development would keep her in this position for the next 11 years. In this position, she drew heavily upon the examples of Mrs. Collins and Mrs. Jones and confirmed her belief in the power of high expectations coupled with empathy. She also called most heavily upon her faith in God. She recalls a former student whose behaviors, while severe, were not rare among her third grade basic skills students:

"There was another little boy who just radiated anger. His body language—the facial expressions, the way he was always threatening to fight someone—just projected anger. He would do anything to distract the class or to avoid work. I went to visit his house once to speak with his mother, who was just as angry. Well, his mother scolded him right there in front of me, but what moved me—what kind of shook me—was that she yelled at him to go make his bed. Now, I could tell that there weren't any sheets on the bed because I could see the corner of it from the kitchen. So that made me think that maybe he had wet the bed that night or something. So that gave me better insight into what this child was going through. It would be difficult for him to come into a classroom and sit down and concentrate on learning something new if this was what he was coping with at home. Did his behavior get better that year? No. But I could understand his situation."

During these years Evelyn taught children who coped with a variety of challenging circumstances, but the important point is that she persistently looked for ways to expand their knowledge and skills. It was important to develop her third graders' academic proficiency, but Evelyn also recognized this as a way of building self-worth in students, several of whom desperately needed a sense of positive accomplishment.

To Evelyn, maximizing students' learning meant creating a classroom environment that supported this aim. In the 1970s classroom libraries were largely unheard of in Plainfield's public schools, yet Evelyn wanted her students to be exposed to a broader selection of stories and poems than those included in students' basic readers. She wanted her students to be able to choose books that interested them, and she wanted them to simply enjoy reading for its own sake. At the time, the Weekly Reader Children's Book Club offered a $5 per month membership plan, and in this way, Evelyn received a hardcover children's book each month to add to her classroom collection. Her husband built display-style bookcases for her classroom library so that students could view books' covers and efficiently locate titles of interest.

At home, Evelyn's basement served as a workshop where she created bulletin-board displays that responded to the needs of her students. An enlarged picture of a brown-skinned woman with one finger pressed to her lips reminded students of the sound produced by "sh". Similarly-hued people and familiar objects offered students reminders of other letter sounds that young readers typically find confusing. A math word problem display reminded students that "difference between" and "fewer than" meant they had to subtract. Wall space meant learning space: it provided an opportunity to increase students' knowledge and offered a chance to build self-worth.

Special projects extended and enriched the daily instruction that Evelyn's students received. She recalls that the students' reading of Roald Dahl's *James and the Giant Peach* provided a memorable highlight of their third grade year; the students were captivated by the idea that a giant peach could be used to cross the Atlantic Ocean. As Evelyn read this story aloud, students enjoyed selecting a favorite character based on the character's personality traits. When the book was finished, the students wrote character descriptions which they displayed on enlarged centipedes, ladybugs, and spiders that Evelyn created in her basement workshop. Evelyn describes the culminating celebration as a day to remember: "At the conclusion, we invited the principal and some of the secretaries up, and we had a peach party. The children brought in some type of peach dessert. Some children brought in canned peaches. One boy brought in fresh peaches that his mother shoved popsicles sticks into – they were peach popsicles, I suppose, and I thought that was so clever! As a class project, we made homemade peach ice cream. I made the custard at home and then brought the custard and the ice cream freezer to school. They took turns cranking that ice cream freezer, and we made peach ice cream. They enjoyed that book, and they enjoyed that project."

Special experiences such as this were paired with rigorous teaching, and students learned.

Our conversations about her years of teaching gave Evelyn an opportunity to survey her career, to reflect on moments of extreme significance, and to share understandings that she developed over longer stretches of time. Her comments about her 33 years of teaching children poignantly and humbly capture the essence of teaching. They offer an inspiring and instructive view of what it really means to work with children.

"Growing up and training to be a teacher, I always put teachers on a pedestal," she says. "I thought it was going to be smooth sailing. I would be the teacher, and the children would automatically learn. Well, that might have been true for my first few years of teaching, but the social turmoil of the '60s and '70s, and the challenges that remained after those years passed taught me that you have to work and plan and expect from children every day. You have to value each child-- no matter what that child's situation is, no matter what the child looks like, no matter how smart he is—you must respect that child. Get to know that child. And work with whatever that child brings to you because when you do, there will always be a way to get that child to learn."

Throughout her years in Biloxi and Plainfield, Evelyn confronted manifestations of significant social and economic challenges. Like so many teachers who are truly transformative, she waged a campaign of excellent instruction and persistently high expectations. Without fanfare, she worked so that children could move on to the next grade having the skills they would need to succeed at that level. Day after month after year, she changed lives. Evelyn committed a portion of her earnings and a large share of her evenings, weekends, and summers to the work of educating children. She viewed it as her responsibility to do so. To Evelyn, it was teaching, just teaching.

I constantly felt (as I suppose many an ambitious girl has felt) a thumping from within unanswered by any beckoning from without.

Anna Julia Cooper

Doreen Hall

By Marilyn Maye

As Doreen Hall reverently unties the wrappings around the glass picture frame, I expect to see a photograph of her with family members, her grandchildren, perhaps. "He's one of my former students," she says, pointing to the impeccably attired military officer, whom she remembered as having been in "the third class down" from the top class in his grade.

Like me, Mrs. Hall was born and raised in Harlem, NYC. We attended the same church for a while and she impressed me as a tough leader with high expectations. Because my godson attended her school, I was aware that she had succeeded in making a difference for black children in the notoriously uncaring city public school system; and, that she had done all of this while being a wife, a mother, and a committed person of faith. She was everything I had gone into education to become.

"It's the requirement of every educator to give a child a valid education, no matter what you think of him. Recognize the individual worth of students, no matter how horrible they are. Just teach them. You never know who he's going to become. I know, because I was miserable in school." She refers to a picture of herself in a 1930s sixth grade class in West Harlem. "I was younger and also bigger than most of the other kids. You can see right away from the picture that I didn't fit in. I was an only child. I had skipped a grade and was not in my social grade. I had no trouble doing the work. I just didn't enjoy school. Most people who know me would be surprised at that; everybody assumes I was a good student, but I wasn't."

The people who assume she had always been an 'A' student are those who only know her as an effective educator and highly-acclaimed principal of Brooklyn elementary Public School 44. Her students were repeatedly featured in the local news media for their outsized accomplishments. In a grade K-6 school with 1200 students of working- and lower-class backgrounds, she became known as a tough leader who could deliver the goods for the children, and could also turn a flailing rookie educator into a star performer who could go anywhere else and be successful. In the 1980s fourth graders in her school had passed the ninth grade mathematics Regents exam. The Regents exams are New York State's high-stakes tests, required in all key subjects in order to earn a college-preparatory high school diploma.

"The College of Staten Island did a study in the 1990s, and determined that, of the youngsters with the worst achievement scores in the first tested grade in my school, we had the highest percentage of those very children who tested on the highest level by graduation time, citywide." Mrs. Hall describes these findings as one of the two things in her career about which she is most proud. "I was extremely gratified. This is how educators in the great cities make the critical difference. We change the children who are personally defenseless. Their only way out is their teacher."

She continues, "My earliest students are long retired by now. I have my doctors, my lawyers, my accountants. I run into them and they tell me about others and I am joyous."

What did she do to gain a reputation as one who could get teachers and students to excel? "I helped them succeed. If they stayed, if they didn't give up, they would get through. They'd get better."

"If you can't take a parent cursing you out when you call to seek her support in getting her child to do what he needs to do, if that's too tough for you, then you need to stay out of the [urban] public schools," she says. "That teacher who comes from the suburbs typically doesn't know what persisting means. 'I can't take it another minute,' she'll say. And I'll say, 'Let's stop and think. This is now January. Let's think about how that class looked in September.

It is better. I'm willing to cooperate with you in any way that I can. But, I want you to know how much progress you and the children have made. Now we're coming into the hardest part of the year. It's coming into spring. And it will be difficult. Don't say it's no different and it's no better.' But, that's because you're working with someone who can't see their own progress. 'These children do love you. They're going to try you, but, they do love you. They don't want another teacher. Let's see if we can make it through.'"

When she was a year old, Doreen's parents moved into one of the historic, black-owned, Sugar Hill-area cooperative buildings, where she now lives. Members of the black migration from the Caribbean in the early part of the twentieth century, her mother and father met while attending high school at night, the only option for black young people of the 1920s. When their only child came along, she walked to school with other black children from Harlem into the section known as Washington Heights, through blocks of houses occupied by sometimes hostile Irish, Italian, and Jewish families. "[The public schools] had to teach us [black and Puerto Rican children], because the classes were mixed ethnically. They couldn't discriminate against us." She recalls that she did not experience the same dedication among teachers toward the nonwhite children, however, as there was for seeing to the success of the whites.

There were exceptions, however. A devout Roman Catholic principal demonstrated a religious zeal for maintaining high standards. "She died before I became a principal myself. But, when I could not devise a strategy to solve a problem, I tried to imagine what she would do. She was the embodiment of integrity, and I was inspired by her." There was also Ms. Aurelis, a twelfth-grade English teacher of Greek heritage, who was "orderly" and "gracious."

Perhaps the longest-lasting influences on Mrs. Hall were her parents, and particularly her father. He eventually opened his own tailoring business in the community after years of working at menial levels in an Italian clothing business, despite the training, skills, and experience he had brought with him from his native land. The boss recognized that her father was as skilled as any of the other tailors, but told him he couldn't give him a tailor position, because the other workers would quit if a black man was assigned at the same level as they. While biding his time to branch out on his own, Doreen's father served for decades as president of the co-op board, governing along with other working- and middle-class blacks, who were not welcome as residents or co-owners in other areas of Manhattan. Such sturdy, well-built, and well-managed buildings are sliding into gentrification today; until recently, Mrs. Hall, served as co-op board president for a decade after her father's death. Her parents had attended nearby City College of New York and amassed 150 undergraduate credits between them, but Doreen was to be the first in her family to earn a bachelor's degree.

With a degree in chemistry, she started out working in a laboratory. She became a wife and mother in her early twenties, with a husband who was well-employed as an engineer. After observing coworkers stricken with immune-system disorders, she realized that being an educator might be more compatible with family life. She got training and eventually a master's degree in education. First as a teacher, then as a professional developer, and finally as a building principal, Mrs. Hall built on the leadership skills and resilience she had acquired growing up in Harlem.

On the way to becoming a school leader, she taught every grade level. "Everyone loves to teach pre-K, kindergarten and first grade. We use material in the children's natural environment. But second, third, and fourth grades are the years when we lose the kids. In the later grades, we move to things that are not natural: the difference between long 'o' and short 'o'. It's not natural. It requires something extra from the teacher.

"By the third grade, the children need more than reading and mathematics. A full curriculum requires a hard-working teacher. Excellent teaching is very hard. You can't spend all day teaching reading. Reading is not a subject. It's a tool to learn a subject. You have to read something. Children can't learn because they have no use for it. …You learn to subtract well when you're doing long division. That's when you learn subtraction. If there's no application, there's no learning. So if you spend two hours a day in reading, and one hour a day in mathematics, I can promise you, those are two things they're not going to learn. It has to be applied. This is part of the job.

"I can show you a perfect example with kids from Tommy's program [she refers to her son who gives private piano lessons in addition to teaching music in public school]. The reason why those children play the way they play is because they are in performance always. He meets them and they teach each other. They have played for the mayor; they play all over. They play for entertainment venues. At my school it was the same thing. At my school it was singing. What kept them going was the touring."

Special competitive events provided opportunities to put other content areas to use. "The children were responsible for an everlastingly long set of words—to know what they mean, how to use them. We used to have contests, vocabulary bees in the auditorium. I'd ask the teachers to make the questions. Here's one word they got wrong all the time: 'elder.' – Here's the word used in a sentence: 'Please don't cut down the elder in the backyard; it's been on the property since so and so.' Then the question is, 'A person in the church, a tree, a this, a that.' They'd yell out, 'A person in the church.' That's the elder that they knew. The teachers would crack up. They'd catch them every year on that one. After a while, they got smart. Eventually they'd learn the other meaning for the word.

"We had the gifted class, the next special one, and the others one after another. Whenever we did the math bee in the auditorium, the kids would be stunned to see that the child who won was not in the gifted, not in the next class, but in the third class down. We'd tell them, "You see, you kids didn't prepare. You are smart, but you didn't study.'"

Mrs. Hall made certain that the teachers worked at a high level of rigor at all grade levels. Over the years, she gathered lesson activities from the most effective teachers, and oversaw the collection of 40 curricular sheets per year for each grade. Teachers had the choice of introducing them at any time during the school year, but they had to have their students complete each of the activities at some point during the year. Completed student work was submitted to the principal, who gathered data on student achievement in each grade and content area. "It enabled me to know what the kids didn't know. I'd send notes: 'It's clear to me that in sixth grade, the kids can't do thus and so.' I wasn't in a gotcha mode. My only job was to see that they got it." The principal would drop by classes from time to time and question students directly about, say, their multiplication facts and other information they should know.

The late Everett Barrett was the college professor and consultant who spearheaded the effort to get the fourth-graders in PS 44 to pass the high-school exam. "I was struck with Barrett's persistence, and, also, here's the beauty with Barrett. His genius was being able to find a method to present something to a kid so that the kid would be able to do it. I saw him show the first graders what the calculus was, and it was no problem. So, if the teacher said, 'Professor Barrett, that doesn't work,' he'd show them another method. He had an endless bag of tricks. It was not hard on them; he did the teaching and left the worksheets. The teachers would watch. He was in the kids' faces. Very hands-on. Demonstrating. The teachers knew exactly how they were supposed to do it. After a while, they got away from being his critic to respecting his work. They knew when he came in they didn't have to do any more work. They could observe him from the back of the room.

"The kids liked it, because it was clear. They like anything that they can learn. If you put it in an orderly way, they'll eat it up. I think if you go anywhere around the world, say a place like Japan, I'm convinced of this, I'm certain in Japan that algebra is about a fifth grade subject. [If they can write Japanese language by second grade.] It's their orderliness; [over there] they don't waste the children's time."

All kinds of enrichment activities kept her students motivated. "We used to do something called the Lunch Bag Workshop. I sent to the parents and asked if they had any special skills that they thought would be good for children. 'Can you knit? Can you crochet? Can you do origami?' Parents would show up. A woman shows up who wants to teach knitting.

I'd write the children in certain grades – all the sixth-graders and all the second-graders. At lunch time, there's going to be a knitting class. You need to bring your lunch. You have to write and tell me why you want to knit. We got boys. We got a big, bruisy basketball player. We got these little second-graders. We'd tell them, 'If you like it, you may stay all afternoon.' You can get that if you've got a big school. You could find the talent pool among the parents and a wide enough range of interest among the students."

"I felt most alone when I knew that it was my last year at school. Other principals were planning for the coming year, my own staff was viewing me as a lame duck, I was recently divorced, one of my sons was giving me a hard time, and I had made no specific plans for retirement."

That was over 20 years ago. Today, at 83, Mrs. Hall can be sighted on the New York City subway system riding to midtown Manhattan and walking (for the exercise) a couple of miles across town to a doctor's appointment, dressed and moving like a person several decades younger. She, along with her business partner, another retired principal, still gets calls from local and nationwide administrators, asking them to talk to new principals and share their insights on school leadership and student achievement.

She credits her faith in God with giving her the strength "to keep on keeping on." "Compelling experiences in answered prayer and God's faithfulness have been a continuing spiritual pattern in my life. I am always stunned at God's steadfast adherence to the promises in His word, no matter how far short I fall." More a person of faith than her parents and other family members were, she is adamant that she finds those on the religious political right today to be hypocritical. "They have not backed a single gracious policy decision. They would be content to see America turned into a third-world country."

By contrast, she'd like to be remembered as a really effective and helpful person. She encourages other educators to try to be effective and to live by the Golden Rule, as difficult as it is to do so.

Just remember the world is not a playground but a schoolroom. Life is not a holiday but an education. One eternal lesson for us all: to teach us how better we should love.

Barbara Jordan

Lillie Ham Hendry

By L. Debra Napier

"Good, better, best, never let it rest, until your good is better and your better is best!" Lillie Ham Hendry truly lives by this motto and shows her personal commitment to the advancement of quality education for all young people, and ongoing, productive service to the community. At the young age of 85, Lillie Hendry remains active in her community of Freehold, New Jersey. Her schedule is as busy today as it was over 40 years ago when she served as the Guidance Department chairperson in the Freehold Regional High School District. She currently serves as the Board President of the Court Street School Education Community Center. The Court Street School faculty members played a significant role in shaping the dynamic person that Lillie Hendry continues to be in her professional and church communities.

I had the good fortune of knowing Miss Lillie Ham (she had not married yet) when I was a student at Marlboro High School, which is one of the six high schools in the Freehold Regional School District. She and her sister Wilma were also good friends of my mother. During the first week of my freshman year she greeted me, reminded me that she and my mother were acquaintances, and invited me to come to her whenever I needed assistance. This made me feel special, as if I had an ally that the other students might not have. As I spoke to my classmates I soon realized that she had extended the same invitation to each of them. That's the kind of person Mrs. Hendry was and still is. Whenever I saw her, she had the same warm smile and words of encouragement for me. She was a role model, especially for the adolescent African-American girls. Mrs. Hendry was always impeccably dressed with her ruby red lipstick and cultured pearls. No matter the situation, she was always pleasant, calm and professional.

My high school experience was in the late '60s, during the era of the civil rights and Black Power movements. African-American students were disheartened, angry, easily excited and often militant in our response to situations. Somehow, I emerged as one of the leaders of the African-American students in our high school and was the person to present our concerns and requests to the administrators. It was during this time that Mrs. Hendry really stepped in to guide me. She counseled me and taught me the most productive ways to convey my ideas to ensure that I'd receive a more positive response from the school administrators. She was not my guidance counselor, but she always made time for me. Mrs. Hendry became my "safe haven." When I found myself angry, discouraged or frustrated due to the ongoing subtle and sometimes blatant discriminatory actions of teachers, students, and administrators, I could go to her for direction. She would help me to see other perspectives and point me in the right direction. It was only after I became an educator that I realized just how diplomatic Mrs. Hendry was: always supporting us (she called us her "little darlings") yet never crossing the line in a way that would offend her Caucasian colleagues. She was one of only three African-American educators in Marlboro High School, and the only minority female. I recall how she would talk us through the situations and then send us to make an appointment with the appropriate administrator, guidance counselor or teacher. One of the requests that the African-American students presented to the administration was to establish afterschool clubs in which the students could learn and share information about our African-American culture and history. The process took many meetings and presentations. Mrs. Hendry guided us through the process and agreed to be advisor to the clubs, both at Marlboro High School and Freehold Boro High School.

In preparing to write this memoir about Lillie Ham Hendry, I interviewed her former students and my high school classmates. Their responses and recollections were the same; they, too, remember Mrs. Hendry as a wonderful role model who was always kind, gentle, caring, and professional. One former student credits Mrs. Hendry with his successful career. He stated that she went above and beyond to make sure that he was prepared to take the SAT and complete the college applications. His parents needed lots of guidance and assistance and Lillie Ham Hendry generously gave of her personal time and expertise beyond school hours. Though Mrs. Hendry has no biological children, she has attended numerous weddings and graduations of her very appreciative former students.

So who is this dynamic woman and where did she learn the skills of diplomacy and professionalism? Mrs. Lillie Louise Ham Hendry was born in Freehold, New Jersey, on April 8, 1929 to her parents, Walter and Lillian Ham. They named her Lillie after her mother (Lillian) and Louise after her paternal aunt. Lillie Hendry was the fifth of her parents' nine children. Her parents taught the older children that it was their responsibility to look out for, and set an example for, the younger siblings. She told me how her oldest sister, Nicy, prepared her for the prejudice and discrimination that she would face once she moved on to the integrated high school. When asked why they were forced to attend a separate elementary school but an integrated high school, Mrs. Hendry explained that Freehold Borough had a larger population of minority students. Therefore, it was financially feasible to build a separate school for the children of the domestic workers and migrant workers who settled in the borough of Freehold. The surrounding districts of Marlboro, Colts Neck, and Howell Township had integrated K-12 schools because there were so few minority students residing in those areas. However, those students had to endure the hardships of discrimination and prejudice in the primary grades. She attended the segregated Court Street School in Freehold Borough, just a few doors away from her family home, for grades kindergarten through eight. As our history books record, the segregated schools for "colored" students had fewer staff, fewer supplies, and books that were handed down from the white schools. In the central New Jersey area, the concept of integrated schools was not accepted by most Caucasian people at that time. If the district could afford to make separate accommodations to appease the majority white population, that's what they did. Mrs. Hendry and her sister spoke about the unfairness of being evaluated using the same state exam that their white peers took when it was common knowledge that they were receiving an inferior education (in terms of academic programs, materials, staffing, etc.) She still remembers how difficult it was to adjust to changing classes each period in high school, because in elementary school they remained in one room with one teacher all day. They did not have instrumental music classes or art and music teachers at Court Street, the "colored" school.

At Court Street School there were four teachers: one taught a combination kindergarten/first grade, the second taught students in grades two and three, the third teacher taught all students in grades four and five. Mr. Read was the principal and teacher of the students in grades 6-8. The teachers had to teach all subjects to a wide range of age and ability levels. Mrs. Hendry has extremely fond memories of the principals and teachers who taught the African-American students during those years at Court Street School. She tells how the teachers lived in the community, knew the parents, and might show up at one's door at any time. Mrs. Hendry also recalls the great dedication that the teachers showed toward the students of Court Street School. They took great pride in the accomplishments and achievements of the "colored" students, always working to help them be the best they could be. Mr. Read was committed to teaching the boys to be courteous, well-mannered young men. There was a teacher who had to ride the train into Freehold each morning. Mr. Read assigned a different boy each week to meet her at the train station, carry her books and materials to the school each morning, and walk her to the train station in the afternoon. Mr. Read, his wife and the other teachers always showed interest in how the students were doing in high school. They reminded the graduates that they were always available for tutoring if students were struggling in any of the classes. It was important to the teachers of the Court Street School that their students could compete with all other students despite the lack of support and resources. On several occasions, Mr. Read wrote letters of recommendation to help students enroll in the "classical" and "scientific" (college preparatory) classes at the high school. Students were grouped according to ability in the high school courses, and the "colored" students were often relegated to the business and manual training course tracks.

Mrs. Hendry talked extensively about the improvements at the high-school level between the time her older and younger siblings attended the high school. Her oldest sister, Nicy, wasn't allowed to participate in the school orchestra at first. However, their parents continued to insist that the children be allowed to do so, and there was no resistance when Lillie, Wilma, and the two brothers graduated to the high-school level. The older siblings paved the way for those coming behind them. Lillie was active in high school plays, the orchestra, and the dance club. She played the viola in the band. Her parents told the children, "Don't ever let me catch you idle." It seems that Lillie never did let them catch her idle. She was always busy! She continues to stay busy at age 85.

Mrs. Hendry credits her parents, the Court Street School teachers, and members of their church (Bethel AME Church) for instilling in her the drive to always do her best, never settle for being second best, and take advantage of opportunities to help others. Her parents were working-class people with nine children to raise. Mrs. Hendry shares stories of the members of Bethel AME Church sending her back to college with her favorite foods and baked goods. When there were special trips that the students wanted to participate in, the church members would take up a collection to help pay the cost of the activities. Mrs. Hendry said, "You got through college and hard times because of the black community that surrounded you with love, acceptance, and support." Her parents and teachers always taught the "colored" students that in order to compete with their Caucasian classmates they would have to be twice as good. Academic excellence was cultivated, expected and supported. Mrs. Hendry shared a funny story about her experience at Trenton State College, where she earned her bachelor's degree in education. While living in Trenton, she attended another AME church in that area. One of the members knew her parents and called them to report that Lillie was seen leaving church before the end of service each Sunday and maybe they should check on her Sunday afternoon activities. Her parents inquired about the situation, only to learn that Lillie was leaving service early in order to catch the last bus back to campus to prepare for Monday's classes. She did not have a car and had to depend on public transportation. This church member certainly meant no harm; she cared for Lillie very much and did not want to see her go astray. It takes a village to raise a child! That was the way of life for Lillie, her siblings, and most "colored" children during those days. Neighbors looked out for the others' children and their property. There was community pride when one of "their" children excelled in a particular arena. The opposite was also true; they did not hesitate to correct a child who was caught in any mischief. Thanks to the guidance, support, and commitment of the concerned adults in her life, Lillie excelled academically and has been recognized for excellence in college studies and her professional career.

Lillie Hendry attended Trenton State College. She recalls her high-school advisor shaking her head as she helped Lillie complete the application, not believing that she would be accepted into that college. However, this was the school Lillie wanted to attend. She had been offered scholarships to attend Hampton Institute (now University) in Virginia and Wilberforce University in Ohio, but she did not want to go far from the close-knit family support that she had always enjoyed. She also knew that she wanted to be a teacher and Trenton State College was well-known for its superb education program.

During her sophomore year in college, Lillie was summoned to the office of Miss Bertha Lawrence, Dean of the Department of Education at the college. Much to her surprise, Lillie had been selected to represent the college at a naturalization ceremony at the State House in Trenton. She was very excited and gives credit to the many opportunities she had for public speaking at her church and high school. Her mother insisted that she wear a hat and gloves and rehearse the speech many times over. She could always count on her parents to reinforce the importance of making a good first impression and being one's absolute best. Lillie relates how supportive her college classmates were. When she returned to campus they asked how she did and told her that they had stopped in the middle of class, bowed their heads, and prayed for her success. Their instructor said that Lillie was the only person who could get the entire class quiet. This was an integrated group of students and Lillie was well-liked by all.

Upon graduation Lillie returned to her community to "serve." She doesn't remember actually hearing anyone verbalize it; however, it was always in the back of one's mind that when one succeeded (i.e., graduated), one came back and served. She applied for teaching positions in Freehold. She specifically requested to be placed in the Intermediate School; however, the administrators offered her a position in Court Street School, where most of the African American students attended, instead. The school had been integrated, but many of the white parents chose not to send their children there. Lillie decided that the district, in which she had experienced so much discrimination, would not continue to subject her to that.

She accepted a position to teach first grade in Hamilton, New Jersey, where she worked for nine years. Her dean, Miss Bertha Lawrence, had recommended Lillie to the Hamilton Township personnel representative who asked Ms. Lawrence to identify a promising African-American graduate to integrate their teaching staff. Lillie remembers the parents' reactions; several asked her where the teacher was. They were surprised when she informed them that she was indeed the teacher. It took a little time but the students and parents accepted her, she developed a good rapport with them, and received very good evaluations from the principal.

Then Lillie received the honor of teaching in England as a Fulbright Education Ambassador. She enjoyed the Fulbright teacher exchange program and it was a good year for her. She experienced a home-stay with a British family who had never had an African-American person in their home before. Lillie remembers that they were loving and unquestioning. They had no preconceived notions or prejudices toward her. She still maintains contact with the family members to this day. As an exchange teacher, Lillie taught in three English schools and lectured in a fourth school. The members of the faculty were just fascinated with the fact that there was an American teaching in their school, not a black American. "I really felt American more than black or African American," recalls Lillie. That was a new experience for her, and she liked the way it felt. One day Lillie's mom said that she might have "grown out of her britches" because she returned to Freehold expecting much more of the surroundings than she had before and diplomatically demanded more from the powers that be. (Now I understand why Mrs. Hendry the guidance counselor could so easily identify with the concerns of the students at Marlboro High School in the late '60s.) She taught one more year in Hamilton after her return from England. Then her mom passed away, leaving her father alone. Lillie helped to build a new home on the family tract, moved back home with her father, and took a position in Freehold Boro School

District. Lillie taught social studies and English in grades 6-8.

Several years passed and Lillie was asked to write the curriculum for the elementary guidance program and became the elementary school guidance counselor, in addition to her full teaching load. "Every eighth grader had to come to my classroom before they could graduate. I made sure that they had the skills that the high school expected, as well as the skills that I had been taught at Court Street School!" remarked Mrs. Hendry. Lillie had internalized the same dedication to excellence that her parents and teachers had poured out to her; she was committed to her job, career and, most of all, to the advancement of quality education for all of her students!

Mrs. Lillie Ham Hendry has received numerous awards for her professional achievements, dedication to academic excellence, community service, and commitment to the work of her church. She continues to be an active member at Bethel AME Church on Court Street in Freehold, where she was baptized, nurtured, and taught the principles of Christian living. Although she has spent most of her life in the Freehold area, Lillie Ham Hendry is well-traveled and a wise woman of the world. She strives to enrich the lives of the young people in her family, church, and community. Mrs. Hendry teaches those fortunate enough to know her to be lifelong learners, set life goals, and to maintain everlasting faith in God.

Lillie Ham Hendry truly epitomizes the important attributes that her parents and those legendary teachers worked to instill in the students at the segregated Court Street School. Until recently she served on the Board of Directors of CentraState Medical Center and the Freehold Borough Zoning Board. She is still active in her church. At age 85, Lillie continues to work to make her good, better, and her better, best!

Every great dream begins with a dreamer. Always remember, you have within you the strength, the patience, and the passion to reach for the stars to change the world.

Harriet Tubman

Penelope E. Lattimer

By Doris R. Lee

I believe people come into our lives for a reason. Each is there to develop or enhance our personal attributes with wisdom, encouragement, support, and love. Some stay longer than others, but no matter how long they stay, they shape who we become. They provide lessons to be learned and to be used wisely over a lifetime.

Penelope Elizabeth Lattimer is one of those people in my life, and she talks about her life in the same way. She believes that whatever she has accomplished is the result of others willingly sharing their time; providing her with opportunities that have broadened her knowledge, understanding, and perspectives; allowing her to grow beyond her own expectations. She expresses her gratitude to each person who has unselfishly given to her by "paying it forward," by generously sharing her skills, understanding, and wisdom with students, colleagues, and friends. She has actively and consciously created pathways for other peoples' successes.

Her life lessons began as a child in Asbury Park, New Jersey. Annie Minor, Penelope's grandmother, taught her how to use time wisely and how to make time for important things such as family, work, community involvement, and practicing one's faith. This meant not just attending church services, but included taking on responsibilities that supported the mission of one's house of worship.

Penelope's grandmother and her mother, Mariagnes, cultivated her love for the printed word and her love for learning by taking her to the library and reading to her until she was able to read for herself. As Penelope grew older, her grandmother used books to help Penelope learn how to understand people and how to overcome adversity as those that she read about had done. Penelope's grandfather, Charles Minor, and father, James Lattimer, provided for the family's financial well-being and were the backbone that held up the family. Her parents worked as a couple to provide enrichment opportunities for their four children, as well as for the family. Penelope, her brother and two sisters were required to study a musical instrument and take dance lessons. Mediocrity was not acceptable. Each child understood the cost to the family in time and money, and the expectation that these opportunities would not be wasted. These lessons Penelope never forgot.

The opportunity to study ballet proved to be life-changing for Penelope. As many young girls taking ballet classes quickly learn, ballet requires time and commitment if one is to excel. Penelope recalls lacking confidence, feeling awkward, and being the worst dancer in her classes for her first five years of study; then it all came together and her talent as a ballet dancer became evident under the tutelage of Dorothy Toland. As Penelope's skills and talent blossomed, she auditioned in New York City at the prestigious School of American Ballet (SAB) and was accepted into the school on the same day. In 1957, fewer than six students of color were enrolled at SAB.

This opportunity came with multiple challenges for Penelope, her family, and her school. Arrangements had to be made for Penelope to travel from Neptune, New Jersey, to New York City for ballet classes; at first, three days, and then six days a week for three years. The Neptune Public School District Board of Education and district superintendent of schools agreed to release Penelope from her afternoon studies so that she could travel by train to SAB studios at 83rd Street and Broadway. Eleven-year-old Penelope learned early on to use her time effectively, completing homework on the train, prioritizing her assignments and deadlines, and being prepared for performance tests. An enduring lesson learned at the highly competitive, performance-based environment of SAB was that good had to become better and better had to become best!

However, when the family moved to Fair Haven, New Jersey, the same early release arrangement with the local board of education was not possible. As a result, Penelope's ballet lessons and performances in New York City ended and her attention turned to New Jersey studies and performances. This change opened other doors. Penelope took a stronger interest in her flute lessons, and she became active in local Girl Scout Troop 199. Penelope recalls high school as a happy time that included international travel with her French teacher, selection to represent Region II of the Girl Scouts of America on an exchange program to Colombia, South America, and flute performances with the marching and concert bands.

I met Penny when I was an undergraduate at Montclair State College. She had already earned a Bachelor's degree in the teaching of French language and culture, and a Master's degree in Student Personnel Services at Montclair. Penelope considers that Montclair was a good choice for her. She was exposed to some of the finest educators in the region. She believes that her lifelong commitments to education and educational leadership were nurtured by those professors. On this mountaintop campus Penelope began to form her philosophy of educational leadership. Ultimately, she placed a high regard on developing learners who are able to think critically and analytically, learners who are curious about the world at large, and who are willing to grapple with speaking, reading and writing in multiple languages. Ideally, these learners will become adults who will integrate the arts into their lifestyle and who are willing to financially support arts education and artists in society, as well as adults who read voraciously and who care about the welfare of others.

I was struggling to fit in at Montclair. I was part of a program, Talent Research for Youth (TRY), designed to help academically promising, economically disadvantaged students succeed in college. At a critical point, Penny took me under her wing and undertook to help me smooth some of the blunt edges of my character. She "pulled my coat tail" to see and appreciate a larger world and my potential place in it. She invited me to ballet performances and restaurants, gently made points of etiquette, offered advice, and over time helped me practice behaviors that would make a difference in how I presented myself and how I was perceived. Penny was not afraid to share her knowledge; she saw it not as a loss but that others' successes were gains for her.

At the same time Penelope felt her personal challenge was to discover how to bring her formal learning, her experience, her philosophy of education, and her early work together into meaningful outcomes benefitting children.

In 1974, Penelope designed and was the first director of the Gibbons School at Rutgers, The State University of New Jersey. The Gibbons School was a demonstration high school, named for the Gibbons campus area at Douglass College where the school was situated. Although the community and New Brunswick Board of Education established the campus-based high school as a reform initiative in reaction to the social disturbances that had engulfed the city and the secondary schools, Penelope saw an opportunity to make academic excellence and student achievement the inspirations to introduce new teaching and learning methods. She incorporated as much of her educational philosophy into the school's curriculum as she could. She hired teachers who shared her vision and passion for "other people's children." She drew students from across the city, creating a population of diverse backgrounds but common goals.

This type of thinking, coupled with the ability to garner public and private funds to support innovative programs, became the cornerstone underscoring the implementation of research-based instructional practices. Classroom practices that are "standard operating procedures" today were considered risky in the early 1970s. Among these practices were techniques such as Learning Styles-Teaching Styles (curriculum alignment responding to data-based review of student progress on local and national tests). Other methods considered innovative in the 1970s included project-based learning (interdisciplinary studies linking teachers and learners in thematic studies). Among the unique features of the Gibbons School was the requirement that students annually completed 50 hours of community service. Another was an emphasis on the importance of the arts. Artists-in-residence spent a month (sometimes staying longer) teaching across the grades, integrating arts education into the core content areas of English, math, science, social studies, and physical education.

Parents/guardians were given letters called Anecdotal Reports. These reports identified the quarterly goals for the course, the objectives that learners attempted or mastered, the learner's strengths and weaknesses, and an indication of what the next learning goals would be. At the end of these Anecdotal Reports would be a grade. College and university admission officers valued these reports because they could read what was taught (not just see a listing of course titles) and how the course was taught, as well as the work that Gibbons learners produced. The culminating work qualifying Gibbons students for Commencement was the requirement that all learners write an academic paper and present the paper at the Senior Recognition Program (Commencement). The faculty's goal was for Gibbons graduates to demonstrate literacy and analytical thinking by their ability to produce academic papers demonstrating excellence in line with what the greater New Brunswick community expected of its high school graduates.

I taught at Gibbons School with Penelope for almost two years and then went on to pursue a career in school leadership. My first appointment as a principal was in Howell Township, NJ. I became the first African-American principal in a district where Penelope's mother, Mariagnes Lattimer, had been the first African-American teacher!

In the 1990s Penelope led a team of educators who designed another demonstration high school for the New Brunswick Public School district. The New Brunswick Health Sciences and Technology High

School (HSTHS) is the only secondary school in New Jersey located on the campus of a teaching hospital. Its curriculum is aligned to core studies of math, science, and literacy, with technology as a learning tool preparing urban youngsters for the broad panoply of careers in the health professions. An essential requirement of learners attending HSTHS is the completion of annual work under the guidance and mentorship of a health professional on staff at Rutgers-Robert Wood Johnson Medical School and Robert Wood Johnson University Hospital. An advantage valued by HSTHS students is the experiential learning that they receive via these mentorships and via summer employment where they see how health care is delivered, how medical professionals interact, and how their classroom studies have direct application to workplace decisions. Penelope advised students not to waste these unique opportunities.

Throughout her career, Penelope has placed high value on factors such as the culture of schools, classroom culture, instructional practice, data use, research use, continuous learning, and the highest quality and diversity of learning experiences for and with educators. She believes that what you don't understand, you won't teach well. When asked about the most important lesson she took from teaching, she says, "I learned the importance of having high expectations for learners, to present the appropriate content for whatever course you're teaching. Don't dummy it down or flatten it out. Do not equate poverty with inability or lack of desire to be an achiever—or lack of interest by parents. Maintain authentic standards and authentic assessment opportunities for the diversity of learners given to you."

She went on to emphasize the importance of preparation and collaboration in one's work. She said, "There is always something more to learn and opportunities will seem to come continuously because of something you did well--often not realizing that others were watching." Even so, she cautioned, "I used to think that preparation and enthusiasm would carry you. That is partially true, but now I know there is denial about what exists and that no matter what, you must keep to your convictions -- whether others join you or not." She concluded, "My advice is to enjoy this important work of educating -- and when you don't, get out of the way."

In her office, Penelope's desk faces a wall where one of her favorite quotes is displayed, a well-known statement from esteemed educator Ron Edmonds, Ed. D. Since the mid-1980s this quote has resonated forcefully with Penelope. It reads: *"We can whenever and wherever we choose, successfully teach all children whose schooling is of interest to us. We already know more than we need to do that. Whether or not we do it must finally depend on how we feel about the fact that we haven't already done so."*

The whole world opened to me when I learned to read.

Mary McLeod Bethune

Dorothy Strickland

By Penelope E. Lattimer

I first met Dorothy Strickland over the telephone. One day I was working in my office at New Brunswick Public Schools' headquarters when my telephone rang. It was Dr. Louise Wilkinson, Dean of the Rutgers University Graduate School of Education. Dean Wilkinson and I collaborated frequently on programs and research so it was not unusual for her to call. What was unusual was her request. Dean Wilkinson was thrilled that Dorothy Strickland was about to sign a contract to join the faculty at the Graduate School of Education; however, Dorothy had one requirement that could be the "deal breaker." Before signing a contract with Rutgers University, Dorothy Strickland wanted to be assured that she would be able to work in the schools and with educators employed by the New Brunswick Board of Education; Louise Wilkinson was calling to ask me to speak with Dr. Strickland and to give her this assurance. I was thunderstruck. Imagine, Dorothy Strickland working in the City of New Brunswick and insisting that she be able to establish roots with the local school district classroom teachers, and school and central office administrators. It was an honor to call Dr. Strickland and welcome her to the New Brunswick Public School District. From that initial telephone conversation to her retirement from the Rutgers University Graduate School of Education, Dorothy shared her knowledge, her time and her work products generously with educators nationally and internationally, but we in New Brunswick and New Jersey know that she always reserves special time to be available to work with us, to inspire us. From this telephone chat a friendship and sharing of professional experiences has continued for more than 25 years.

A few months passed before Dorothy Strickland and I met face-to-face. I remember how calm and pleasant she was. Already she was well known as a reading guru.

Even as a child, Dorothy was influenced by educators. She loved to read. Although her mother did not share her passion, and her father preferred reading daily tabloids to reading books, both "indulged my passion," as Dorothy puts it. The local librarian, Mrs. Luex, was the one who particularly encouraged Dorothy's love of reading. "Whenever I entered the library she would greet me as if she had been waiting for me all week. She would reach under her desk and pull out a very special book that she had been saving just for me. Perhaps most important, she made me feel so very special. We shared a love of books and reading. Little did either of us know that I would someday be the State of New Jersey Professor of Reading."

Another childhood experience that influenced Dorothy's life was a middle-school trip to the Paper Mill Playhouse in Millburn, New Jersey. "We were taken to see a Gilbert and Sullivan operetta— something that was completely foreign to us. Needless to say, I was absolutely enthralled. There were real people on the stage. They sang when they talked to each other and they sang songs as well. They had on lavish costumes and they all seemed to know what to do every moment. It was very different from the movies and I loved it." At the time, Dorothy had a job as a "mother's helper" in Millburn, so she began saving some of her earnings so she could see more shows at the theatre. "I never shared this with my friends, lest I be seen as odd," she recalls. "But I could not get enough of the theater then or since. My interest and love of the theater persists to this day. It was, of course, the school that introduced me to something that my parents never would have. The Paper Mill Playhouse was so close, and yet, so very far away."

One of Dorothy's most profound career-related challenges came even before her career as an educator was formally launched, in 1954. She was attending Newark State Teachers College and preparing for her junior practicum, one of two six-week field experiences before graduation. Students selected several districts where they would like to be placed, and then were assigned to a district based on these choices. Dorothy was assigned to the Bloomfield district, along with some other students from the program.

"About two weeks before the practicum was to begin, the students who had been assigned to Bloomfield were called in and told that they would be reassigned to other locations," she remembers. "Of course, we were all disappointed and perplexed. It seems that the administrators in Bloomfield had learned that one of the students was a Negro and Negroes were not permitted to participate in this kind of experience in that town."

Rather than let one of their students be singled out, Newark State Teachers College pulled all of its students from the Bloomfield placement. "I, of course, was devastated and, I am sorry to say, a bit ashamed that it was my fault that the other students had to be reassigned. I was an honor student who made the Dean's List virtually every semester... my first thought was to, somehow, blame myself." Despite her disappointment, Dorothy had a very successful practicum in the Elizabeth school district. She concludes, "For better or worse, I kept most of my frustration and bewilderment inside and moved on to work very hard in my new placement. But still, to this day, I search for answers."

Dorothy's second six-week field experience was a teaching assignment during her senior year. This experience led to her first teaching position, in the East Orange school system. "I was thrilled. I was the second black teacher (Ruth Jacobs was the first) in that town. My photo was in the newspaper. Needless to say, in 1955, it was a very different town demographically." Her first assignment was to teach fourth grade. "East Orange was a wonderful place to begin my career...my colleagues were very supportive and helpful. My interest in the teaching of reading really emerged during this time. Although I was considered a competent teacher, there were a few children who did not appear to be thriving as well as I thought they should. I felt they were much smarter than they appeared or than their test scores indicated." As a result, Dorothy decided to pursue a master's degree with a focus on the teaching of reading. "Studying for that degree opened up a whole new world for me. The work was grounded in the teaching of reading for all children. However, it also focused specifically on reading problems and learning disabilities." Once she obtained her degree, she became a certified Learning Disabilities Specialist in New Jersey. The degree also led to a position in East Orange as a reading specialist.

One of Dorothy's fellow teachers in the East Orange district also taught at Jersey City State College and recommended her for an adjunct professorship in the teaching of reading. "The course went well, or so I thought. However, no one came to observe me and I did not receive a call or letter afterwards regarding my work. I, of course, was perplexed and disappointed— particularly with myself. At the end of July, I received a call from the department chair asking if I would be willing to teach full time at Jersey City State. I was elated and, lucky for me, the folks in East Orange were very encouraging."

Looking back, Dorothy notes, "As I reflect on my journey, it occurs to me that I have been guided by a strong belief that it is important for me to do the very best job I can in the many roles I undertake, whether personal or professional, and then give a little bit more. My effort will be noticed. I don't have to tout it, just do it. I confess that I realized this pretty much in retrospect since virtually all of my career moves have been determined by invitations that were based on my past performance."

Her next such invitation came from the department chair of the Early Childhood Department at Kean College (formerly Newark State Teachers College, Dorothy's alma mater). She was asked to design and teach courses focused on teachers working in pre-kindergarten through third-grade settings. During her six-year stint at Kean, Dorothy worked her way up to become department chair. She also continued her professional development and pursued a doctorate at New York University. As she attended conferences for organizations such as the National Council of Teachers of English and the International Reading Association, she met and networked with colleagues. "[My mentors] counseled me to attend sessions in my areas of interest and introduced me to key individuals and committee members. Soon, I was invited to serve on committees. I was awed to actually meet the names on the 'reference lists' of the professional books I had been reading and the papers I had been writing for my classes. I discovered that these were people who were extraordinary in their intellect and background knowledge about the things I cared about, yet they were open to new ideas and respected the ideas of others. I was treated as if my ideas were worthy, as well. All of this made me want to learn more and to make a contribution to the field." As a result of her involvement in professional organizations, more opportunities developed; service on committees, publications, and finally, a chance to run for the presidency of the International Reading Association, which she won.

Dorothy's work as a leader in her field led to an invitation to apply for a position as a tenured full professor at Teachers College of Columbia University, one of the top institutions in the field. She applied and got the job. However, she had just been approved for a full professorship at Kean. Dorothy remembers, "What I hadn't realized is that there was a specification that I must remain there for two years. This, indeed, was a dilemma. I decided to request a waiver from the requirement, but I was certain that if I asked my department chair, it would be denied. So, I really bit the bullet and went directly to the president of Kean. He could not have been more gracious and kind. He made it clear that he would not stand in my way." After a few years, Dorothy was named Arthur I. Gates Professor of Education.

Dorothy's next big challenge came from New

Jersey's World Class Scholar Initiative, passed by the New Jersey Legislature under Governor Tom Kean. This gave department chairs the ability to hire world-class scholars to their institutions, offering an endowed chair, a research stipend, and staff as perks for the positions. Rutgers University offered Dorothy one of these positions, leading to a very difficult decision. "The invitation was enormously enticing, yet it was also very troubling. Teachers College had been very generous. They had also been very vocal in their requests for me to stay. Also, I loved it there and [wanted to] maintain my ties with members of the faculty and with Teachers College Press. After a year of decision-making, I agreed to go to Rutgers. However, I would teach a final fall semester at Teachers College and move to Rutgers in the spring. I also agreed to teach an adjunct course at Teachers College during the spring semester as part of the transition."

Dorothy's professional activities, particularly with the International Reading Association, led to an international reputation as a leader. "I served as Chair of the World Congress on Reading in Hamburg, Germany; as a member of a Commission on Literacy in China, and other advisory committees in Singapore, and the Ivory Coast; and as a presenter at conferences in Argentina, Chile, Paris, Canada and many other places." One memorable trip was to the then-USSR in 1980. "I arrived in Moscow, picked up my luggage, and waited to greet the two women who were supposed to meet me at the airport. After waiting for what seemed like a very long time, two women who had been lingering in an area not too far from me came over and asked if I was Dr. Strickland. It occurred to me that in all our correspondence...we had never mentioned that I was an African American. After getting over the shock, the two women were extremely gracious throughout my stay. One served as my guide and interpreter. The other served as 'minder,' something that was very common during the cold war."

Looking back on her career, Dorothy credits mentorship and a regular routine of professional activities for her success. "My primary mentor [at New York University], Dr. Bernice Cullinan, was extremely generous and supportive of me both as an individual and as a doctoral candidate. I once asked her how I could ever repay her. Her answer, 'The best way to repay me is to simply hand down the magic.' At first, I wasn't sure what she meant, but it became clear as I found myself in the position of helping to guide students in their professional lives. The challenges will always be there, yet knowing that someone who truly cares is also there may provide the very best support for facing those challenges. Perhaps most importantly, that person serves as a model for helping others to face their challenges as well."

Trust yourself. Think for yourself. Act for yourself. Speak for yourself. Be yourself.

Marva Collins

Gloria Jean Tunstall

By Valarie W. French

"It's all about the children. I am a kid advocate."

Gloria Jean Tunstall ("Call me Jean") lives by a simple rule: "If it benefits kids, let's do it. If it doesn't benefit students first, change it. " Her mission over more than 40 years in public education has always been to make things better for kids. Her career has been a series of decisions to expand her role in creating positive environments for learning. And, if she looked around and saw that the decision-makers did not include women or minorities, she stepped into the breach.

I met Gloria Jean Tunstall in 2003 when I began working in the Trenton, NJ public schools. But before I met her face to face, I knew her name. Everyone did. She was a veteran elementary school principal in the district and the president of the Trenton Administrators and Supervisors Association (TASA). Her first words to me were a compliment, which is Jean's way: to make a personal connection that can form the basis for working together. She approaches

71

everyone – from kindergarten students, to staff, to parents, to colleagues – as members of her extended family, deserving of her attention and her care.

Jean Tunstall always wanted to be a teacher. She figured out early in life that she wanted to work with children and set her sights on achieving a degree in education. She was the first in her family of six sisters to go to college. She recalls that her parents wanted their daughters to finish high school but did not insist on college. They said, "Do what you like, what is comfortable, what makes you happy." Jean finished high school in Harrisburg, PA. She explained that there were two public high schools in the city. She attended John Harris, but most black students attended William Penn. She recalls that as a very small minority in the predominantly white high school, black students socialized and took part in activities together (and partied with William Penn).

Jean believes the teacher who had the strongest influence on her development as a teacher was her high school Spanish teacher, "Senorita". Jean does not remember addressing her any other way, but does remember that this teacher commanded her admiration and respect. Jean believes that because of the foundation provided by that teacher she can still read and understand Spanish and draws on it when talking to parents and students in her school, a bilingual center. Her willingness to speak in Spanish and ask for help with vocabulary delights her students. Jean said they will give her a 'thumbs up' and assure her that she is getting better. She smiled and said, "That [connection] brings me joy."

After her high school experience, Jean wanted a predominantly black experience for college. She had only heard of Howard University (DC) and Morgan State College (MD), but when a neighbor came home extolling the advantages of his college, Jean enrolled in Central State University, a historically black college in Wilberforce, Ohio.

Jean graduated from Central State in December 1970. For a year and a half after graduating from college she taught fifth grade in Harrisburg. It was "frightening and exciting." She was the only African American teacher, but it was a young staff and they helped each other, "so, I didn't feel inadequate." She remembers taking the textbook manuals home on weekends and reading them carefully before preparing lesson plans. She recalled a lesson she learned from her first principal. She asked the principal to send a custodian to her classroom to move a table. At the end of the day, the principal appeared in her room and moved the table herself. Jean said she decided then that if something ever needed to be done in her classroom, and she could do it, she would.

In 1972 as a newlywed Jean moved to Trenton and began teaching fifth grade in the public schools. I asked Jean what it was like. The de facto segregation of Trenton elementary schools had been reversed and "white flight" into the suburbs around Trenton was rapid. But for Jean, it was about the kids, in particular, exposing her students to life beyond their community. She took students ice skating, to the ocean, to a mall so that they could ride an escalator. She remembers in great detail taking a class to a local restaurant's lunch special. The meal was $5.25 per person and each child had to have $6.00 to cover tax and tip. Each child was expected to order from the menu, calculate the bill and tip and anticipate the change. Jean felt her students needed a wider experience than "ordering off the placemat at McDonald's. I liked exposing students to another way of life."

She also recalls investing time beyond the school hours in her students, putting them in her car and taking them out to eat or to her home. She said she believed -- then and now -- that when she could form relationships with her students outside of school, they had better attitudes in the classroom. That was her approach to classroom management. She shudders remembering that in those days there were 30-35 students in a class, and the curriculum called for between 5 - 7 reading groups. Each group represented a different reading level with a different basal reader. "It seemed like we taught reading and language arts all day long, moving from group to group." She noted that today, using guided reading strategies, there is no need to divide students into so many groups.

To her class she preached personal development, personal responsibility and self-discipline at the start of every school day, and then read to them. She remembers that she read *Charlotte's Web* aloud several times a year to illustrate personal responsibility and sacrifice, and that it paid off in many ways, including being able to dismiss her class from the third floor, confident they would exit without incident, which was a blessing for a teacher nine months pregnant!

"Everything I did was with kids." Over the years, Jean started community-based activities to benefit children. For four summers she ran a day camp from her home. This was a solution to several problems: one, vice principals – as well as teachers-- worked on 10-month contracts and needed employment in the summer and, two, there were no summer programs for her pre-school daughter. The day camp solved both problems and attracted children from the city and the bordering suburbs. In the early 1980s Jean was one of the original mentors in an academic preparation and enrichment program, SMILE (Science & Math – Interesting and Learned Easily), sponsored by Mercer County Community College for aspiring Trenton middle and high school students. The program provided homework help and brought in inspirational speakers including noted neurosurgeon, Dr. Ben Carson, and NFL Hall of Famer, Reggie White. Active in her sorority, Alpha Kappa Alpha, Jean currently works with middle school girls in an emerging leaders program.

I asked Jean what she is proudest of in her career and with no hesitation she answered, "Knowing I made a difference in students' lives." She sat back and shook her head slightly. Many former students have gone on to college, but some became substance abusers and two have died. "When I meet [former students] it's enough to know that they're alive and have jobs," she said. Jean runs into former students all the time in the city. She laughed that all of the Hispanic officers on the city police force seem to have been her students. She said she is sometimes worried when she runs into them, wondering what they remember about her classroom, but invariably they say, "Mrs. T, because of you we're where we are now!"

As a successful teacher, why did Jean Tunstall decide to become a principal? She says she saw the principalship as a way to make sure more people did right by kids. "I wanted to be a principal because I wanted to ensure students were exposed [to outside experiences]. As principal I could influence that. It's important to think outside the box. School trips were my exposure when I was in school and I wanted that for children in Trenton." She felt that as a principal she could have more influence over the learning environment and what happened to children. In preparation, and because she is a lifelong learner, Jean earned Master's degrees in urban education and school leadership from The College of New Jersey.

Jean was the principal of Cadwalader Elementary School for 17 years. Cadwalader's population is 100% eligible for Chapter I services and 80% eligible for free/ reduced price lunch. In 2005 the school was recognized as a Governor's School of Excellence for sustained improvements in student achievement, one of only two schools in Trenton to achieve this distinction. Achieving the state recognition and treating her entire staff to dinner at a local restaurant is one of her favorite memories of Cadwalader. She says, "It was won-der-ful!" but there are other memories that reveal how Jean managed her school. The Human Resources director, a powerful friend and advocate, asked her to hire his daughter, a newly certified teacher, for an opening at third grade. Jean had a great deal of respect for the director, and maybe owed a favor or two, but she said, "No, not at third grade. That's my testing grade!" She concludes, "He later said he respected me more for that." Her focus is always on the kids. Jean noted, "People outside of education don't understand. We don't push paper, we work with human beings."

"When I decided to become a teacher I wanted to teach social studies, but districts didn't have elementary social studies positions, only secondary. Elementary school was where I wanted to be, but I wasn't patient enough for kindergarten or first grade. It's hard to teach children to read! So, I taught fifth grade and all I cared about was fifth grade. But, one year my principal asked me to take a fourth grade class. I made him promise the assignment would only be for that year. But you know what? I learned a lot that year. I realized that it was important for fifth grade teachers to know what students had learned in fourth grade, and what would be expected of them in sixth grade, kind of like backwards design. As a principal I want teachers to talk to each other about what's coming before [the grades they teach] and what's coming after. I've grown so much in wanting to know how to do it right for kids."

When Jean Tunstall was appointed a principal in 1986, she joined the Trenton Association of Supervisors and Administrators (TASA). She describes the leadership at that time as a "boys' club." No woman administrator had ever won election as TASA president, so Jean decided to run. She won and remained president for seven years. When she was appointed an Assistant Superintendent in the district in 2005 she resigned from TASA, but when all assistant superintendent positions were eliminated from the budget a year later, she returned to a principalship and was re-elected as president of TASA in 2010.

Making things better for students also means forging relationships beyond your own schoolyard. As president of TASA, Jean became active in the NJ Principals and Supervisors Association (NJPSA). She was disappointed and frustrated by the low participation of minorities in the organization. "So much information does not get to urban districts." So, Jean joined the leadership team of NJPSA and eventually served as statewide president in 2005-6. She is the first African American woman to serve as president of NJPSA. She is still actively involved in the organization and now serves on the board of the NJPSA Foundation for Educational Administration (FEA). Jean has also served on the NJ Department of Education Board of Examiners for about 12 years. She explained with a smile that she sits on the certification side of the board, not the legal side. From this position she has learned a lot about the certification process in the state, information she has been able to share with aspiring administrators.

Shouldering responsibility, setting goals, doing a job well started early for Jean Tunstall. The family moved to Harrisburg from Memphis, Tennessee in 1959 when the Air Force reassigned her father to Ansted AFB. Jean remembers the drive from Memphis to Harrisburg vividly. It was dangerous for blacks to travel or to stop along the road. "We couldn't stop, so we had shoebox lunches – chicken, bread, and cake. That's what we all always packed in those shoeboxes, isn't it? We couldn't drink much because we couldn't be sure we could find safe rest stops. I didn't realize how difficult it must have been for my mother, driving across the country at night with four little girls and pregnant with my sister."

Of six daughters she was the one who spent the most time with her dad. Her father eventually owned two gas stations in Harrisburg and had a government job after retiring from the Air Force. Jean's job in the house was to bank the fire in the coal furnace each night while her father was at work. It was an important job to make sure the fire was damped and smoldering steadily because that was the only heat. But she didn't like housework. "My sister liked housework because it gave her time to read, but I wanted to be out of the house. I would ask my dad, 'take me with you. Don't you need help at the gas station this afternoon?" Indeed, Jean believes her mother was probably the first woman to operate a gas pump in Harrisburg, and eventually Jean was the second. Whenever her parents traveled she was put in charge of collecting the business receipts and accounting for all of the transactions at the gas stations while they were away. Her fondest memories are of "being with family". Family sometimes included additional "uncles" and "aunts" in the house; these were family and friends her parents sheltered when they came north to find work.

Now, at Washington Elementary School, Jean says her mission is – and will remain – creating a safe environment for students that is conducive to learning. She recounted an issue from her first year as principal at Washington. A few parents were in the habit of entering classrooms with their children, or popping in throughout the day to talk to them. While parental involvement is an important element of the learning environment, Jean felt this parental behavior had the potential to create unsafe conditions. She disallowed it, insisting that parents sign in to the office before entering classrooms, but she also created a monthly parent meeting as a place for parents to discuss their concerns and students' needs. She observed, "It is incumbent on us to protect students, then educate them. I need to create an environment that I can control for kids. I get satisfaction when I see kids happy."

Further, she is insistent that teachers treat students with respect. When she arrived at Washington she felt that teachers were not convinced that all students could learn. She told a story of a teacher encountering a student in the school office, whom he recognized from another school in the district, and describing the child's disruptive behavior there in lurid detail. Jean stepped in and said simply to all in earshot that this was a new school and a new opportunity for the student to succeed. She reports that the student is fitting in, doing ok. To help teachers sustain high expectations for all students, each week she assigns a story or article for reading and discussion by staff that shows how a teacher changed a student's life, such as a New York Times article about Judge Olly Neal who credits an English teacher with changing his life's trajectory.

Jean has been a leader in the Trenton public schools for 40 years. The most important lesson she has learned about teaching? "Kids just want to feel loved, that someone cares, that you're there for them." Looking back she says, "I tried to do it the way I thought was right. As educators we have a moral responsibility to educate children and keep them safe." She would advise new administrators to do the same: "Have a strong will, know who you are, and always do what is right for kids – not for the grown folks. Everyone won't like your decisions, but if you know in your heart that you are doing it for the right reasons, stick with it. Do it for the kids."

I've learned that people will forget what you said, people will forget what you did, but people will never forget how you made them feel.

Maya Angelou

Bessie Wade

By Penelope E. Lattimer

Like many little girls, Bessie Wade liked "playing school" with her dolls. She would line them up every day and read to them. Her early childhood playmates gathered together to play counting games such as, "5-10-15 Red Light...STOP!" "We wanted to be smart in school," said Bessie.

Bessie Wade's mother had a third-grade education and was a cook in a private home in Augusta, Georgia. Bessie's father died at age 26 in a car accident. Bessie's mother encouraged her daughter to enjoy school and she worked to provide a stable home for Bessie and herself. Perhaps because Bessie's mother had such a limited education, she was anxious for Bessie to be an earnest learner. Bessie remembers her mother asking her frequently, "What do you want to be when you grow up?"

The Augusta schools were segregated when Bessie began her formal education in the 1930s. She entered Haines Institute School for kindergarten and first-grade studies. Bessie remembers her mother telling her, "Your name goes with you." These words stayed with Bessie throughout her elementary, high school, and college years of studying and developing socially. Later, as a classroom teacher, Bessie would say to her students, "Your mother did not send you to school to just sit...you are not an ornament. You can't just sit here." These powerful words made it clear to students and parents that Bessie Wade held high expectations of academic achievement for all youngsters in her class.

When she was in second grade, Bessie walked to school each morning with her teacher, Miss Philpart. Bessie remembers, "Miss Philpart was a role model. Walking with her every day was very special. She inspired me to be an educator." As they walked, they talked. "Miss Philpart would talk to me about things in general such as how beautiful the day [was]. She asked me about memorizing poems. I recall my first poems were 'The Cow' and 'My Shadow' by Robert Louis Stevenson." At this point, to my delight, Bessie recited a stanza from "My Shadow":

"One morning, very early,
Before the sun was up,
I rose and found the shining dew
On every buttercup;
But my lazy little shadow,
Like an arrant sleepy-head,
Had stayed at home behind me
And was fast asleep in bed."

She smiled, "Memorizing those poems taught me to appreciate the seasons of the year and the time of day." I smiled, too, because I remembered reciting these poems as a child with my mother and grandmother after learning them in Bessie Wade's classroom.

As a product of segregated schools, Bessie Wade believed that she had to make pathways for success for other people's children. She was born and raised in Augusta, where her mother and stepfather had to pay for her to receive a high-school education. Augusta did not have free public high school for African-American children. There were three private schools that accepted African-American children. Bessie's parents were able to pay the monthly school fees so she was able to complete high school. Bessie remembers her teen years as being good ones. She attended church and Sunday school, and sang in the choir. Her family was Southern Baptist but she had friends who were Methodist and Catholic.

Bessie attended college at Benedict College in Columbia, South Carolina. She entered in 1946 and graduated in 1950. During this time, Bessie's lifestyle was broadened immensely. "I met many young men who had returned from fighting in World War II," she recalls. "Some of them became educators and advanced to being school principals. I had Caucasian and Oriental [Asian] instructors. Our music teacher was excellent. We would have teas at college; I learned how to take tea, how to dress wearing hosiery, hat, and gloves." Social etiquette was an important part of

Bessie's personal development and an important component of the curriculum at Benedict College. This included strict adherence to school rules such as Sunday church service in the morning and vespers service in the evening.

Benedict College professors mentored their students and were excellent role models for Bessie, who knew that she aspired to a career in education. Among the teachers who impressed her most were her geometry and trigonometry math teachers; Mrs. Robinson, her English teacher, who helped to develop her reading and writing skills; and her French teacher, Mrs. Douglass. These professionals helped Bessie to think carefully about taking the career path to education. She also drew upon her memories of her own school days. "School was wonderful," Bessie says. "When I was in college and preparing to be a classroom teacher, memories of wonderful school days contributed to my enthusiasm to be a professional teacher. I never considered being an administrator."

The summer before Bessie's senior year at Benedict College, she lived with her aunt in New York City. William Wade was about to start his senior year at City College of New York, majoring in chemistry, but he was working part-time as an elevator operator during the summer. The two began to date and continued their long-distance relationship via weekly letters when Bessie returned to South Carolina to complete her degree. After they graduated in May 1950, William and Bessie got married at Mother AME

Zion Church in New York City on August 19, 1950.

After living in Manhattan for a year, the Wades moved to the Jersey shore. William got a job as a chemist at Fort Monmouth, while Bessie accepted a teaching position in the Asbury Park Public School District. This was the beginning of a 38-year career in the district. She started at the Bangs Avenue School, where Hyland Moore was the principal. Bessie recalls, "My entire career in Asbury Park Public School District was very enjoyable. I had parents who cooperated with me." While William and Bessie were working and pursuing advanced studies in their respective fields, they had two sons, Bertram and Jonathan.

Bessie's top priority in teaching was to create a safe space for her students. "Children are fragile people… Each year, I knew that I needed to develop a culture of classroom kindness to help my children feel safe and secure to do their best work and to be acknowledged for it [by me and their families]." She also reached out to others in the school and in the community to support her students' learning. "It was important for me to become acquainted with the entire school staff and the community-at-large so that I could continually help youngsters to see that school and learning were exciting. I wanted my children to be confident learners. I knew that the more they learned, the more tasks they could do, the better they would feel about school and themselves."

Another priority for Bessie was to continue her professional development. "Having Kean College (now University) and Monmouth College (now University) nearby gave me many opportunities to study with prominent researchers and educators," she says. "I knew that being an educator meant that I could not stand still. If I wanted to be an advocate for my students, I needed to be prepared to help them with 'their moment in time.'" She particularly remembers taking classes with Dorothy Strickland. "I remember Dorothy Strickland as an outstanding professor at Kean College who taught courses in reading. Dorothy Strickland was some instructor! She taught us techniques for working with children. She taught us how to embellish our reading classes, not to just sit with the teacher's manual on our lap." Her hard work paid off when she earned a Master of Teaching degree in Elementary Education from Kean College.

Bessie used a variety of methods to keep her students engaged. "I wanted to teach my children using different methods," she recalls. "I began by integrating math into reading instruction. I wanted children to be able to visualize the number concept. For instance, I would illustrate the sameness and the difference between the word 'three' as it is written and used in a story and the numeral '3'. Or, I would draw houses and put numbers (instead of people) in the houses to demonstrate the concepts of place value and re-grouping."

Bessie continues, "As my confidence grew and with more years of classroom experience I began to diversify my instructional methods; for instance, I never took the teacher's manual and just used the lesson for the day. I examined the manual to find lessons for different students." She incorporated her love of poetry into her teaching as well. "Every day I read poetry to my children. My philosophy was to use poetry and other literature to illustrate that man doesn't live in the world alone. We have to know how to live in connection with nature and how to live with people." To illustrate, she recited a verse from Robert Louis Stevenson's poem, "The Cow":

"The friendly cow all red and white,

I love with all my heart:

She gives me cream with all her might,

To eat with apple-tart."

She used singing to teach her youngest pupils, and emphasized visualization when teaching cursive writing by telling students that the letters were dancing.

Bessie's lengthy tenure and success earned her the respect of her peers. "Administrators always saw something good in my classroom. Often they sent young teachers to me for guidance," she remembers. By the time she stopped teaching in 1992, she was giving in-class support for slower learners in kindergarten, first, and second grades.

For most of my life I thought that Bessie Wade was my first teacher. One day when I introduced Mrs. Wade to friends and colleagues as my first grade teacher, she gently corrected me and told me that she was my *second* grade teacher. Regardless, Bessie

Wade has had a profound, life-long influence on me. She was the first teacher to ask my mother if I could bring my ballet slippers to school and demonstrate classical dance forms for my classmates. It was an opportunity to share these new experiences of the larger world with others. My mother trusted Mrs. Wade and her decisions; they bonded and remained friends for many years. I have been fortunate to have had, not only my mother but, Bessie Wade supporting me throughout my life.

When asked for advice she would give to today's teachers, Bessie emphasizes the need to create a safe space for learning, the importance of ties to the larger community, the necessity of continuing professional development, and the need to know one's subject areas well. While noting that technology can aid teaching, she warns, "...don't become over reliant on it. Please take time in this world of technology to start with 'hands on' learning experiences that make the big idea of the lesson concrete and something that the learner can visualize and relate to. Do this fundamental work with the learner before placing him or her in front of a computer or calculator." She sums it up by saying, "Teach every child in your classroom as if that is your child. Have high expectations for each child's achievement. If you don't do this, the child loses out."

"I would like to be remembered as a teacher who was not afraid of challenges," she concludes. "From my students I would like to be remembered as a teacher who instilled pride and joy in learning."

Authors

Penelope E. Lattimer, Ph.D. directs The Rutgers Institute for Improving Student Achievement and The New Jersey School Development Council at Rutgers, The State University, Graduate School of Education. She was formerly New Jersey State Assistant Commissioner of Education. She was Assistant Superintendent for Curriculum and Instruction, and Principal of The Gibbons High School in New Brunswick, N.J. Her teaching certification is in French language and culture. She lives in New Brunswick, New Jersey.

Valarie W. French, Ed.D. is an educational consultant specializing in program design and evaluation. She has served as Special Assistant to the Commissioner of the NJ Department of Education, Special Assistant to the Superintendent (Trenton, NJ Public Schools), Director of Curriculum at The College Board, and as a Vice President for Assessment of the National Board for Professional Teaching Standards. She lives in Pennington, NJ with her husband, Michael Randall.

Marilyn C. Maye, Ed.D is associate professor in Educational Leadership at New Jersey City University. Her research is in public school leadership and in mathematics education. She consults nationally for schools, school districts, and professional development organizations. She is a founding trustee of the Bronx Charter School for Better Learning in New York City. She has served in leadership positions for the New Jersey Department of Education, Englewood Public Schools, New York City's Department of Information Technology and Telecommunications; she has taught mathematics at Queens College of the City University of New York and in the New York Public Schools. She is the author of *They are Men and Not Gods*, and *Stone of Help: Ebenezer – the First Fifty Years*, and co–author of *Orita: Rites of Passage for Youth of African Descent in America*. www.DrMaye.com.

L. Debra Napier, M.Ed is an educational consultant in the areas of special education and language arts literacy. She is a certified LDT-C and elementary teacher. During 32 years in public education Debra was a classroom teacher, school administrator, Supervisor of Humanities, and Director of Whole School Reform. She also worked for Educational Testing Service (ETS) as a Scoring Director, training teachers across the country to assess portfolios for the National Board for Professional Teaching Standards.

Mary McGriff, Ed.D. is co-chair of the Literacy Education Department at New Jersey City University, where she teaches and conducts research related to English language arts and teacher professional development. She is the author of *Teacher Identity and ELL-Focused Content Area Professional Development* and co-author of *Addressing Adolescents' Need for Voice and*

95

Interaction. Dr. McGriff is a former school principal and middle school language arts teacher. She lives in Flemington, New Jersey with her husband and sons.

Doris R. Lee, M.Ed is an educational consultant for Educational Information and Resource Center (EIRC), located in Mullica, New Jersey. Her work includes providing professional development for school administrators and teachers as a trained facilitator of McREL's research on Balanced Leadership, Classroom Instruction that Works (CITW), and McREL's Principal Evaluation System. Her experiences include 33 years in public school education, 22 years as a school administrator.

31677746R00069

Made in the USA
Charleston, SC
25 July 2014